Praise for *Is That You, Ruthie? The Play*

'Aunty Ruth's story doesn't shy away from the harrowing and heart-breaking, yet, it is a truth told with light and shade, laughter and tears, made only more visceral with Leah's talent for bringing stories to life on stage.' —**John Kotzas AM, Chief Executive QPAC**

'Amid the tears and the laughter, Purcell captures the resilience and indomitable spirit of a woman who has defied Australia's oppressive racist policies.' —*Arts Hub*

'While a full-on dramatic adaptation of Ruth's story could create a six-part mini-series, this 90-minute one-act play is the perfect encapsulation. And, apart from a cuppa with this 94-year-old Queensland legend herself, there's no better way to meet Ruth than to see her play … a story of our recent history that every Australian should see.'—*Stage Whispers*

'Purcell and Hegarty share the same creative agenda: both women blend the personal with the political through autobiographical storytelling and the power of witnessing.' —*The Conversation*

'An important recognition of the past as much as it is a haunting inquisition that demands we listen.'—**Kate Cantrell, USQ**

Leah Purcell AM is an internationally acclaimed, multi-award-winning playwright, actor, producer, director and a proud Goa-Gunggari-Wakka Wakka Murri woman from Queensland. *The Drover's Wife The Legend of Molly Johnson* was Leah's debut feature film, which she wrote, directed and co-produced as well as starring in the leading role. Her previous adaptations of the original Henry Lawson short story, *The Drover's Wife*, includes the multi-award-winning theatrical play and the best-selling book. Leah's theatre directing credits include *Brothers Wreck, Don't Take Your Love to Town, Stolen, The Story of the Miracles at Cookie's Table, Radiance* and *The 7 Stages of Grieving*. She is also the best-selling author of the anthology *Black Chicks Talking*.

First published 2025 by University of Queensland Press
PO Box 6042, St Lucia, Queensland 4067 Australia

University of Queensland Press (UQP) acknowledges the Traditional Owners and their
custodianship of the lands on which UQP operates. We pay our respects to their Ancestors
and their descendants, who continue, cultural and spiritual connections to Country.
We recognise their valuable contributions to Australian and global society.

uqp.com.au
reception@uqp.com.au

Cover design by Madeline Byrne / UQP
Cover photograph by Peter Wallis / Wallis Media
Author photograph by Marnya Rothe
Typeset in 11/14 pt Adobe Garamond Pro by Post Pre-press Group, Brisbane
Printed in Australia by McPherson's Printing Group

 **Queensland Government** University of Queensland Press is supported by the Queensland
Government through Arts Queensland.

  University of Queensland Press is assisted by
the Australian Government through Creative
Australia, its principal arts investment and
advisory body.

A catalogue record for this book is available from the National Library of Australia.

ISBN 978 0 7022 6927 1 (pbk)
ISBN 978 0 7022 7250 9 (epdf)
ISBN 978 0 7022 7251 6 (epub)

University of Queensland Press uses papers that are natural, renewable and recyclable products
made from wood grown in well-managed forests and other controlled sources. The logging and
manufacturing processes conform to the environmental regulations of the country of origin.

Aboriginal and Torres Strait Islander readers are respectfully cautioned that this publication
contains images/mentions of people who have passed away.

Is That You, Ruthie?
The Play

Leah Purcell

This play contains references to the removal of children from their families, the effects of displacement, and the ongoing impacts of institutionalisation for Aboriginal and Torres Strait Islander people.

For assistance with reuniting with family, Link-Up operate reunion services in each state to members of the Stolen Generations (aiatsis.gov. au/family-history/you-start/link).

The following organisations provide support, resources, asssistance and counselling:

Yarn 13
13 92 76
13yarn.org.au

Head to Health
1800 595 212
headtohealth.gov.au

WellMob
wellmob.org.au

Beyond Blue
1300 22 4636
beyondblue.org.au

Contents

My past is nothing more than the
trace that I have left behind.
What drives my life today is the energy
that I generate in my present moment.

—Dr Wayne Dyer, from *Your Sacred Self*

Two hearts breaking
Silently waiting to touch
No one hearing the sounds.
Unable to see the tears.
Across the large room
Their silence pounds.
A message of love breaks.
Their hearts – explode.
Not hearing
Yet knowing
I am here.

—Dr Aunty Ruth Hegarty

Introduction by Leah Purcell

The process of bringing this play to life carries immense cultural and traditional significance. For First Nations people, the passing down of stories is essential – it's how we have survived and evolved for millennia. Our traditions may be interrupted, our culture fractured, but our stories endure. They live within us and are ours to tell.

These stories must be told to bring understanding and awareness to non-Indigenous people and remind our younger generations of what our Old People went through. This play honours their experiences, provides a platform for their voices, and offers hope for those who've been removed, stolen, or lost.

When I sat down to write this introduction, I couldn't help but reflect on the play's structure. It's deeply rooted in the Blakfella way of storytelling. We start by establishing who's who and explore the interconnectedness of the characters. Then we begin, sometimes deviating into side stories (what we call 'scenes within scenes' in the play). These deviations always have meaning, and everything eventually intertwines in the story's fabric until the conclusion. I'm proud to say this play is a proper Blakfella way of telling a yarn – and, as it turns out, so is this introduction.

I've known Dr Ruth Hegarty, Aunty Ruthie, since I was a little girl. She was friends with my mother when they were growing up in Cherbourg, but it was more than friendship – they were family. My grandmother, Daisy, my mum's mum, was family to Aunty Ruthie's mother, Nanna Ruby. They were cousins – Gunggari mob from Mitchell, Queensland.

Nanna Daisy's family is complicated to trace because she was stolen when she was about five years old. She was taken from her mother and traditional lands and sent to Cherbourg, formally known as Barambah Mission. Daisy was lucky, though – family from the main camp on Barambah Mission came to claim her, so she never entered the dormitory system set up at Cherbourg to train Aboriginal girls for servitude and cheap labour. It was around 1910 when my Nanna Daisy was placed on the Barambah Mission.

Now, let's jump to the early 2000s. I was on my way to the Gold Coast to act in an American production called *Beast Master*, which was being shot at Warner Brothers Studios. I played the Black Apparition – a character with red eyes and a hoofed hand that could throw fire. My family were with me, including my man, mate and manager, Bain Stewart, who's also managing director of Oombarra Productions. He loves a good book, and had found a copy of Aunty Ruthie's autobiography, *Is That You, Ruthie?*, in a bookshop discount bin. He bought it for me, maybe because the blurb mentioned Cherbourg and he knew of my family connections there, which continue to this day.

As we drove to the Gold Coast, I opened the book and started reading. I couldn't put it down. I laughed, cried, and finished it that same night.

I turned to Bain and said, 'I have to find Aunty Ruthie.'

Through the Blakfella grapevine, I tracked her down. I was lucky that Ruth's mother, Nanna Ruby, was still alive, so I made time to visit them after filming.

The visit was emotional. I was searching for information about Nanna Daisy and wanted to know if Nanna Ruby knew anything about her immediate family. We cried together, laughed, spoke and sang language. Nanna Ruby called out my mother's and nanna's names. She wailed for them, said she could see them in me, and shared everything she could remember.

Years later, researching for this adaptation, I was given an old, filmed interview with Nanna Ruby. The interviewer kept pressing her for more profound answers in the footage, but it wasn't in her to give him what he wanted.

She changed the subject and said, 'But I can talk about my cousin, Daisy'. Her face lit up with a beautiful smile.

Watching this, I was almost in tears, excited to hear more about my nanna's life. But then the tape cut out. The footage was damaged – no picture, no audio. I cried again.

After that first visit, I told Aunty Ruthie I wanted to do something with her book. She said that would be lovely, and we left it at that.

Years passed, and then in 2023 she called me and said, 'It's the book's twenty-fifth anniversary, and I'm ninety-three years old. When are you going to do something with this book?'

I told her, 'Aunty, give me three months and I'll have a first draft of a play idea for you.'

Bain pitched the idea to QPAC's CEO, John Kotzas, and he said, 'If Leah's writing and directing, we're in.'

As I wrote, I realised I couldn't tell the story from Ruth's perspective alone. I had to tell it from both hers and Nanna Ruby's. Ruth's fifth book, *Buthalangi: A Maranoa Woman*, about her mother's life, came at the perfect time. At the heart of the play is the journey of a mother and daughter, forcibly separated (by the government policy of the time, the *Aboriginal Protection and Restriction of the Sale of Opium Act, 1897*, known as 'The Act'), and finding their way back to one another. I often thought about my Nanna Daisy and wondered what it would have been like if she'd had the chance to reconnect with her mother. Maybe, subconsciously, I wrote this play for her, too – a way of imagining her story.

⁓

To me, Aunty Ruthie is a mentor – someone I look up to and admire – a woman of determination, drive, wit and resilience. We share so much in common. This production has helped me grow in my craft, showing me the maturity and knowledge I've gained over my thirty-three years in the industry thus far.

I approached this project with a sense of urgency, diligence and efficiency. My mother is no longer here to see this, so to hear Aunty Ruthie say how proud she is of this play, and what I've done to bring her story to the stage, means the world to me.

It is a gift to have Aunty Ruthie here to share her story. At ninety-five years young, she continues to inspire me – not just as an Elder but also as a fellow writer.

⁓

I'm proud to bring this story to the stage and even prouder that this publication will ensure it lives on for future generations. I hope to see many productions – interpretations that expand it from a two-hander to an entire cast. I want this story to reach as many people as possible.

My dream for this play is to bring about understanding, change and hope for a better, more inclusive future. Truth-telling is the foundation of growth and healing.

This process has been a personal milestone for me as a writer and director.

Western way, my craft is sharpened.

Blakfella way, Women's Business – I am initiated.

I am a Storyteller.

I proudly and sincerely gift to you, *Is That You, Ruthie? The Play*.

Altjeringa yirra Baiame.

Noolla nagarla,

Yantell-our-oo.

—Leah Purcell AM, Writer–Director

*Ruth Hegarty (left) and Leah Purcell (right) at rehearsals
during the first production of the play.*

A Message from Dr Ruth Hegarty

Writing the Dormitory Girls story was always something I had to do, and when I finished *Is That You, Ruthie?* I had fulfilled the promise I made to my dormitory sisters and to my children to understand my early life.

To have Leah Purcell take my story and adapt and translate it to stage has given it new life and sounds beyond my imagination. I am a storyteller, but she is a creative artist, and together we have built something that will hopefully resonate and educate the wider community about the rules and regulations that dictated every aspect of mine and my mother's life under 'The Act'.

My legacy is that my people, and in particular my dormitory sisters, are recognised and rightfully given their place in Australia's history, not as the poor cousins, but as a group of people who endured in a time of oppressive racist policies that tried to break our spirits and turn us into imitations of the white society.

—**Dr Aunty Ruth Hegarty**

Notes on the Play

In Queensland, the *Aboriginals Protection and Restriction of the Sale of Opium Act 1897*, known as 'The Act', controlled the lives of Indigenous people for the next sixty or so years. It gave power to white 'Aboriginal Protectors' to forcibly remove Aboriginal and Torres Strait Islander people onto dedicated land reserves and restrict their movements, including separating families and allowing children to be removed from their parents. The legislation was also used to remove their basic civil rights and determine where they worked, how much they were paid, and how much of their own pay they could access. The children in these institutions received almost no education, trained in servitude, and their labour was exploited. The effects on Aboriginal family life were devastating and continue to resonate profoundly today.

~

This play features a non-linear storyline and incorporates stylised movement in certain sections, including dance routines.

This play is bookended with the mature Ruth and what triggered her to write her story. We start out with shared scenes with mother and daughter, before exploring their solo journeys. We bear witness to both of their experiences, chronicling the day they separated, their time enduring the hardships of dormitory life, and their challenging work lives. While there are parallels in their journeys, one narrative delves into more detail, eliminating the need to recount similar experiences in the alternative narrative. The paths of mother and daughter eventually intersect again as they attempt to reconcile and collectively confront their haunting memories. The structure of this play imitates their actual life's path.

Archival footage and personal family photos are projected onstage to add depth and context to the narrative.

Guides for pronunciation and translations for language are indicated in [brackets].

CHARACTERS

Two First Nations female actors.

ACTOR 1
(forty to sixty years old)

- Ruth/Ruthie/Little Ruthie –
  Munya [Mun-*'u' as in 'nun'*-ya]
- Narrating – indicated as
  ACTOR 1 – formal voice
- Gunggari person
- Doctor
- Judy
- Inmate
- Rita

ACTOR 2
(twenty to forty years old)

- Ruby – Buthalangi
  [Buth-tha-lan-gee]
- Narrating – indicated as
  ACTOR 2 – formal voice
- Marcia
- House Parent/Old Granny
- Station Master
- Boss's Son
- Mistress
- Inmate
- Clerk

Ruby Duncan's exact age is unknown. She had a bush birth and, as a result, the day, month and year of her birth were never documented. According to Ruth Hegarty, author of the novel, *Is That You, Ruthie?*

(UQP, 2003), Ruby, known as Buthalangi, was born under the flowering Kurrajong tree. Her age was estimated to be nineteen when she arrived in Cherbourg in February 1930. At that time, Ruth was six months old, having been born in August 1929.

～

The actors will double as various characters within scenes, requiring versatility in voice and physicality.

The play includes direct address to the audience, alternating between character and narrator modes:

Narration is indicated as *ACTOR 1* or *ACTOR 2*. When performing as a narrator, your tone should be more formal and distinct from your character's voice.

Quotation marks around 'character dialogue' signify scenes within scenes where characters interact. In these moments, 'other characters' may also feature within the scene. Their presence should be conveyed through the actor's voice being 'thrown' – to suggest they are offstage, distant or approaching the main action. At times, one actor may fully embody another character within the scene.

SETTING

This play is set between 1930 and the present day.

Strategically placed in the upstage area is a concealed freestanding panel. It is adorned with various-sized pieces of paper resembling the canopy of a Kurrajong tree. There is a ramp in front of the panel, allowing performers to use this area to perform on, and to enter the stage from behind and in front.

On the stage, four file boxes are strategically positioned around a much-loved highbacked armchair. One of these boxes is open, and the paper inside appears to flutter upwards, mimicking the appearance of a tree trunk. Another box holds a notepad, loose papers, a tea mug, pens, and delicate wooden peg dolls meticulously crafted to resemble miniature figures and dolls.

Two platforms, one measuring 300 mm and the other 600 mm in height, are used to delineate the dormitory area. Their surfaces gleam like highly polished floorboards. On the taller platform is an old-fashioned iron bed with a barred head and footrest, reminiscent of vintage dormitory beds. Adjacent to the bed is a bedside table featuring a landline phone and a lamp.

As the audience enters there is an old hurricane lantern on stage, it is lit.

PART I
Reasons to Write

Scene 1

The lantern begins to flicker, we hear in Gunggari language the 'Maranoa lullaby'. The night sky projected. The lantern goes out. Stage goes dark.

Ruth (Actor 1), sixty-six years old, appears on stage. She wears a dressing gown and heads to her bed, reciting a prayer.

RUTH: Now the day is over, night is drawing nigh.
               Shadows of the evenin', spill across the sky.
               Jesus, give me … calm, and sweet repose.
               With thy tendresse blessin', (*sigh*) may my eyelids
               close …

She reaches her bed and attempts to kneel …

               'Lord, my knees are not what they used to be, so,
               I'll just say, goodnight.
               And Lord knows, my knees have been put to the
               test.'

Ruth gets into bed, as the prayer is finished by young Indigenous female voices – a memory.

YOUNG FEMALE VOICES (VO):
               (*Reciting*) Glory to the father, glory to the son.
               And to the blessed spirit while all ages run.
               Now the day is done.

Once Ruth is settled, she turns the lamp out by clapping her hands. A giggle in the dark (night light).

RUTH: '(*To herself*) Technology, true. Bless my daughter, Lord, for buyin' that fancy light.'

A moment of darkness (night light) and silence, then the phone rings.

RUTH: '(*To herself*) Now, who on earth could be ringin' me at this hour of the night?'

She claps again. Lamp light turns back on.

RUTH: I reach for the phone.

She takes the receiver, the phone stops ringing, still addressing the audience.

A call at this hour of the night could only bring bad news.
My family know, unless it's life or death,
any phone call can wait for the mornin'.

RUTH: 'Hello?'

AUNTY HAZEL (VO):
'Is that you, Ruthie?'

RUTH: I pause for a moment before answering.
I smile.
Here I am, sixty-six years of age,
and in an instant
I'm back to my childhood,

4

dormitory days.
That voice and those very words –
'Is that you, Ruthie?'

I'm tempted to stay in the memory.
I reply.

'Yes, it's me.'

AUNTY HAZEL (VO):
      'Aunty Hazel here. I just wanted to let you know that Dulcie died.'

RUTH: Oh, dear.
          Just as I thought.
          Bad news.

AUNTY HAZEL (VO):
      'Remember Dulcie? Dulcie from the dormitory days.'

RUTH: 'Of course,'
          I say.

          Who could forget Dulcie.
          She was one of us.
          A dormitory girl.
          How could I ever forget one of the sisters?

          A real character.
          A paraplegic.
          Born that way.

Like the rest of us,
spent her early years in the Girl's Dormitory.
Barambah Aboriginal Settlement.
Known as Cherbourg these days.

Dulcie determined to be accepted.
Her independence was a thing to see.
The dormitory didn't cater for the disabled.
Dulcie taught herself to walk on all-fours.
Raised herself up off the ground.
Her arms stretched behind,
bent knees to hold her bottom off the ground.
Using her hands and feet,
she had great corns on them.
We all admired her though.
Always determined.
Always unassisted.
Her own special place in our hearts.
Memories come floodin' back.
Vivid memories of days gone by.

Memory – subtly, young female children's voices.

Almost hear the voices of us children.
What a long time ago that was.

Ruth gets out of bed and grabs her dressing gown.

Image of Barambah Single Mothers and Children's Dormitories.

RUTH: Sixty or so of us girls.
          Grew up together in the dormitory.
          Not knowing, why, we were there.

Never darin' to question.
Interned at such a young age.
Institutionalised for reasons known only to the
government.

We were treated identically.
Dressed identically.
Our hair cut, identical.
Our clothes and bald heads were a giveaway.

Image of dormitory girls in their calico dresses with shorn heads.

We were Dormitory Girls.

Scene 2

Actor 1, narrates in a formal voice, talks to the audience.

ACTOR 1:   Ruth Hegarty, nee Duncan, her story begins in
1930.
That was the year her family moved to the Barambah
Aboriginal Settlement.
She was six months old.
A very fair-haired, fair-skinned child.

Ruby, Ruth's nineteen-year-old mother, enters.

Baby Ruth left the west with her mother.
(*Indicating Ruby*)
Buthalangi [Buth-tha-lan-gee] or Ruby,
or Ruby Anne as she came to be known.

Ruby's parents, George and Lizzie Duncan.
George, a Kamilaroi man,
brown snake totem.
Chinese father.
Lizzie, full blood Gunggari [Goong-gar-ree],
possum totem.
Baby Ruth's mother,
Buthalangi or Ruby or Ruby Anne,
eldest of eight.
She was nineteen at the time.
Ruby remembers quite vividly, everything,
that led to her family's decision to leave the west.
Southwest Queensland, Mitchell.
Out Roma way.

A hard decision.

A necessary one for the survival of the family.

Ruby – Buthalangi.

Ruth – Munya [Mun-*'u' as in 'nun'*-ya].

Buthalangi and Munya's story.

A mother and daughter's journey back.

Scene 3

~ 1930 ~

Ruby now holds a crying swaddled six-month-old baby in her arms
(a piece of calico wrapped to look like a baby swaddled).

RUBY: (*Indicating herself*) Buthalangi [Buth-tha-lan-gee] …

                (*Indicating to the swaddled crying baby in her arms*)
                My baby daughter.
                Six months old.
                Ruth Elizabeth.
                My mother,
                called her Munya [Mun-*'u' as in 'nun'*-ya] –
                first grandchild.

                We come by train.
                Mitchell to Brisbane.
                Brisbane to Murgon.

                Truck from Murgon Railway station
                to Barambah [Ba-ram-ba] Aboriginal Settlement,
                3.6 miles.

                Side of the road, possessions unloaded.
                My siblings: Eric, fourteen; George, twelve;
                Duggie, ten; Glen, nine;
                Forrest, four; sister Jean, two;
                and the newborn baby boy, Leslie.
                Waiting silently.

I want to freshen up Ruth,
not easy to keep her quiet.

Ruby anxiously sings quietly in Gunggari the 'Maranoa Lullaby'.

'Mar-ra warren no, mar-ra wothen no.
Mar-ra wothen no. Mar-ra warren no.
Baby go to sleep, in your bed of bark.
Mamma watches you. Mamma watches you.'

Word of our arrival got out, fast.
A few familiar faces to welcome us.
Gunggari [Goong-gar-ree] people – forcibly
removed from the homeland.
What a welcoming sight.

Actor 1 becomes a Gunggari Person who welcomes the family.
Ruby starts to sing in language again to quieten a crying Baby Ruth.

RUBY: (*Singing softly*) Mar-ra warren no, mar-ra wothen no.
             Mar-ra wothen no. Mar-ra warren no.'

GUNGGARI PERSON:
             'Garra [Gar-ra] dhaa [dar] ngalga [null-gan–nar].'
             [No speak language.]

             'Boss comin'.'

RUBY: And they're gone.

             The Superintendent,
             Mr Semple.
             Tall man with greying hair.

Severe looking.
Scottish accent.
Spoke with great authority.
Paperwork in hand.
He, the powerful white man.

He knew our names.
The family's history.
Is Baby Ruth and I written there?

'I'm only here for a little while.
Help my parents settle in.
Seeking assistance.
The Depression.'

No one's listening.

'To the Camp.'

I hear the Superintendent say to my parents,
the youngest two in tow.
Accommodation there, they *might* find.
'Otherwise build your own out of whatever you
find.'

The family's separation.
No explanation.

Baby and I, escorted,
by native police,
to the hospital.
Examination.

Actor 1 becomes the Doctor and does the examination – ears, eyes, teeth.

RUBY: And the—

DOCTOR: 'All clear.'

RUBY: —is given.

         Then ...

The Doctor tries to take the bundle of cloth (representing the swaddled baby) from Ruby. The cloth begins to unravel, the Doctor begins to tear it. One piece ripped and thrown, Ruby runs to retrieve it, holding it dearly.

         My brothers to the Boy's Dormitory.

Another piece ripped and thrown. Ruby runs to retrieve it and holds the two pieces dearly to her heart.

         My parents to the Camp.

Finally, the third strip is thrown. Ruby scampers after it.

RUBY: Myself and Baby Ruth to the Women's Quarters.

Ruby tries to piece the cloth back together.

         Like, an old rag ... my family ripped apart ...

Ruby continues to try and put the torn cloth back together.

ACTOR 1:   Ruby's last memory of that fateful day.
           The day when all their lives changed, forever.

RUBY: Torn apart. Family broken.

ACTOR 1:   All in about an hour … this family's freedom gone.

           What happened to the paperwork that said:
           Only seeking assistance during the Depression.
           The Great Depression causing depths of poverty for
           all people:
           Aborigine, migrant and white.

RUBY: 'The Mitchell Police Sergeant said,
           "Just for a little while".'

ACTOR 1:   Ruby wanted to scream.

RUBY: 'I'm only here for a little while.
           Help settle my family in.
           Why is my family being split up?
           Please!
           I should not be here!'

ACTOR 1:   But she remained quiet.
           To speak like that, Blackfella no right.
           The control, absolute.
           Her fate sealed.
           Ruby no recourse.
           No way to communicate with Frank.
           Frank Saunders, her betrothed.
           Her baby's father.

*Actor 1 becomes Judy, Ruby's Murri friend from Micthell. Ruby holds
the swaddled baby as Ruby and Judy talk.*

RUBY: 'Judy, Frank paid five pounds for a back room at the
          hospital.'
          Proof of his good intention.
          Not allowed inside, but medical assistance given.
          For the birth of his daughter, Ruth Elizabeth.'

Ruby is proud and happy. She gives Judy a nurse of Baby Ruth.

JUDY: (*To audience*) Despite the racist policy,
          his daughter will have a birth certificate.

Judy fusses over the baby in her arms.

RUBY: 'Judy, Frank proposed.
          On his return from the Drove,
          we are to marry.'

*Judy is happy for Ruby. They embrace. Image of Frank Saunders
appears.*

ACTOR 1: (*Indicating image*) White man to look at.
          But research found his grandmother, Blackfella.
          Frank always hung around the Yumba.

Image of the Yumba. Image of the Maranoa River.

          Carted water from the Maranoa.
          Charging four shillings a load.
          But, Ruby, no way to communicate where she went.
          Where she was sent.

Later,
Ruby learnt,
Frank tried to find them,
but told, they'd died.
Frank's search ended.

Scene 4

The two narrators set the scene.

ACTOR 2:   It's 1986. Ruth's fifty-seven years old.

ACTOR 1:   At home, 4 Wavey Street, Zillmere.

ACTOR 2:   I, Ruby, make an announcement.

Pause.

RUBY: 'You should find your father.'

Ruth in shock, flips over the bed.

RUTH: Imagine my shock!
            Well, you just saw it.
            (*Indicating the flip over the bed*)
            When for the first time,
            in my life, *she* mentioned I had a *father*!

            Cheekily, I reply,

            'Do I have a *father*?'

            Dumbfounded.
            How could my mother keep a secret like that from me?

            I did vaguely remember,
            hearin' her whisper—

17

Ruby bends, as if addressing a toddler.

RUBY: 'He will come for us.'

RUTH: I didn't know who *he* was!
            His name was never mentioned!

            'What's his name?'

RUBY: 'Frank Saunders.'

RUTH: 'How am I supposed to find, Frank Saunders?'

RUBY: 'You'll find him.'

Beat. New memory.

RUTH: It took me a while to muster the courage to contact
            my father.
            It was by phone.

FRANK (VO):
            'Hello. Frank Saunders speaking.'

RUTH: 'Hello?'

            I was silent for a moment, letting my thoughts
            steady.
            Not sure what I was going to say next.

            'I'm … I'm … I'm your … I'm Ruby Duncan's
            daughter.'

FRANK (VO):
        'Yes. You are Ruth. Ruth Elizabeth.'

Pause.

RUTH: He remembered my name after all those years!
           Made me feel ... good.

           Our first visit.
           I went to his house.
           Toowoomba.
           Joe.
           My childhood sweetheart.
           My Camp Boy.
           My husband now, drove me.
           We sit.
           In the car.
           Waitin' for my courage to come.

           I remember back to my dormitory days.
           Not one of us had mothers, let alone fathers.

           But I would imagine,
           what my father might look like.

Beat.

           Tall, handsome, rugged, tough.
           John Wayne!

           Then, this old man,
           not much taller than me,
           opens the front door.

Not aware that I was seated in the parked car outside.

I turn to Joe.
'That can't be my father.'
And he said,
'It is. Now get out.'

Beat.

I was very uncomfortable.
Frank, a stranger … arms out ready to embrace me.
But I couldn't.
He spoke a lot about his past.
How he tried to find us.
Told me everything.
I wished I listened.
My mind, racin'.
Relieved, when my husband came to collect me.

Beat.

I was very sad for Mother.

Nineteen-year-old Ruby appears with the swaddled six-month-old Baby Ruth in her arms.

RUBY: (*Singing*) Mar-ra warren no, mar-ra wothen no.

           'He proposed.'
           (*Singing*) Mar-ra wothen no. Mar-ra warren no.

           'Showed his good intentions.'
           (*Singing*) Baby go to sleep, in your bed of bark.

'To marry after the drove.'"
(*Singing*) Mamma watches you. Mama watches you.

'… He will come for us.'

Memory dissolves.

Scene 5

~ 2004 ~

*Seventy-five-year-old Ruth takes a stack of government 'personal file'
papers about her mother and has a read.*

RUTH: (*To audience*) In my research to find information on
            Mum,
            taken aback to find ...

            ... the 'Order of Removal'
            for the family *and me*.

            (*Reading to self*) 'Came of their own accord'

Image of the Removal Order appears.

            (*Reading to self*) Mitchell to Barambah from the
            Department of Native Affairs,
            February 1930 ...
            ... destitute?

            (*Reading to self*) Four cart geldings,
            A creamy mare – (*To audience*) value three pounds
            each.
            One old wagonette, harness,
            four horses – (*To audience*) valued at fifteen pounds.
            A saddle, and bridle – one pound.
            (*To audience*) In total, thirty-one pounds.

            Grandfather George's property.
            Proving he was well-off.

22

Grandfather George, self-employed.
Looked after the family very well.
A residential address in Mitchell – Mary Street.

An era of the self-made Aborigine.
Getting ahead.
Playing the whithu [width-thoo] – whiteman –
at his game.
Winning.

Ruth reads, tapping at the papers, emphasizing what she is reading.

'A good worker'
'Temperate habits'
'Quite capable'
'Protecting himself and his family.'
But whithu play dirty.
Mentality all wrong.
Divide and conquer.
Position of power to put us down.
Policy turned us into fringe dwellers,
broken Blacks,
Ruled by 'The Act'.

But *that* Depression, that was sweeping the world,
everyone in dire circumstances …

The smarts and character of my grandfather,
Mr. George Duncan did not come into the decision.

*A distressed nineteen-year-old Ruby appears with an agitated
swaddled Baby Ruth in her arms.*

RUTH: Because of our cultural identity …
          we were officially removed.
          Placed in the care and protection of the Queensland
          government.

Beat.

          In hindsight, Ruby should have stayed in Murgon.
          Next train back to Mitchell.
          Because what happened in just those few hours,
          after our arrival at Barambah …
          … all our lives, changed.
          Just like that.

Ruth claps her hands. Lights out.

Part II
Ruby

Scene 6

~ 1930 ~

Images of the Dormitory. Nineteen-year-old Ruby fearfully walks the space, a sleeping, swaddled Baby Ruth in her arms.

RUBY: The Dormitory, a two-storeyed building.
Top floor, everyone slept.
Divided in two.
Lattice-work divide.
One section housed the women –
single mothers and babies.
The other side,
two wards for the little girls and big.

Largest place I've ever lived in.

Ruby, fearful.

RUBY: Matron Pascoe.
The Matron – white authority, hard taskmaster, very strict.
And her Aboriginal House Parent, Old Granny,
ordered to carry out Matron's discipline.

Image of a row of single beds, almost identical to the bed on stage.

Tonight, shows me where to sleep.

Ruby arrives at a single bed.

No longer will I enjoy the bush,

or the Yumba,
or the Maranoa River,
where I fished, swam and played.

No longer could I decide,
where I went or who I saw,
my freedom gone.

This new world, demanding –
the drills. The many rules and regulations.

Nineteen years old, a mother myself.
But suddenly a child again.

Actor 1 comes on stage as one of the timid inmates. Ruby introduces herself.

RUBY: 'Buthalangi. Gunggari.'

                   I was born when the Kurrajong tree was in bloom.
                   Ngiya warala guila ngunggana [Nigh-ya war-lar-la
                   goo-ill-a nung-ga-nah].

                   The flowers were yellow and scented.
                   Wuba yala, badyuringa [Wub-bee yella bud-due-
                   rin-ya].

                   I was my father's pride and joy.
                   Ngiya ngadyu yabu budyirangunga [Nigh-ya nud-
                   gue yub-boo bud-due-rung-gunna].

                   Buthalangi – a Maranoa woman.
                   Buthalangi – Gunggari Ambi [Buth-tha-lan-gee
                   Goong-gar-ree um-bee].

Actor 2 assumes the white Matron's voice.

'Speak English, conform!'

Inmate snaps to attention.

Buthalangi – no more.
Ruby Anne Duncan – Barambah inmate.
Identification card number – 1DC/D291

BOTH: I, a ward of the State.
Under, 'The Act' -
*The Aboriginal Protection and Restriction of the Sale of
Opium Act, 1897*
This law, to protect and care …

New day. Ruby and Inmate make up the bed, immaculately.

RUBY: The large house was strange.
With lots and lots of women and children.
My fear of the unknown is growing.
Each new day brought about its own fears.
No sight of my family in several days.

I clung to one hope –
that Frank,
Ruth's father,
he proposed.
We were to marry after the drove …
'He'll come for us,' I'd whisper.

But, day by day.
Time passed.

And the rules!
The drills!
The bells –
in the morning.
Get up.
Go eat.
Go to work.
Go to bed.
Every day the same.

(*Smiling*) And looking after Baby Ruth.
Thank goodness she's with me.

Ruby enacts choreographed stylised work routine.

Scrubbing floors.
Washing clothes.
Cooking.
Cleaning.
Earning our keep.
No one was allowed to sit –
to work, to work, work, work.

Inmate joins her, and they repeat the words and action of the work routine.

BOTH: Scrubbing floors.
Washing clothes.
Cooking.
Cleaning.
Earning our keep.
No one was allowed to sit –
to work, to work, work, work.

ACTOR 1:   She very much regretted her decision that day.
            To accompany her parents to this place.
            Where she and Baby Ruth didn't belong.
            Ruby,
            no authority over herself
            or her daughter anymore.
            Matron Pascoe making all the decisions now.

Actor 1 re-joins the work routine as an inmate. The stylised cleaning action continues. Ruby does a variation of it.

RUBY: As I slowly got to know the other female inmates,
            and understand what they were saying,
            my heart sank.

Images of other young mothers and their babies in the Mother's Quarters. Actor 1 becomes the various inmates.

INMATES: 'Keep Ruthie on the breast for as long as you can.'
            'Keep her a baby.'
            'She becomes big girl and able …'

BOTH: 'Matron will take her away.'

ACTOR 1:   Ruby wondered,

RUBY: 'What kind of people would take your child away?'

Beat.

RUBY: It was a losin' battle.
            Ruth crawled early.
            Ruth started walking early, too.

Ruth, in a hurry to grow up.
The thought of losing Ruth, too much.
My thoughts of Frank, almost a dream now –

Image of Frank Saunders projected and fades.

I was sure he *wasn't* coming.

Scene 7

Images appear of men in lines, waiting to be picked for work. Men employed. People at the ration shed with sacks of food. Image of the Boys' Dormitory projected. Image of young boys.

Images appear of Barambah Aboriginal Settlement sign, mud map showing the camp, streets, houses/gunyas – the home-made shelters on the settlement.

ACTOR 2:   The people, from all over Queensland.
All removed from their Country.
Cooktown.
Birdsville.
Thargomindah [Tharga-min-dah] tribe,
and the Burnett Blacks.
Butchulla [But-choo-lah].
Hawkwood.
Sundowners.
Kullilli [Colourah-lee].
Wakka Wakka [Wok-ka Wok-ka].

The 'Camp', divided into tribes and localities.

Top Camp. Middle Camp, Bottom Camp and China Town.

Gunggari – from the Maranoa district, Western murries.

RUBY: That's me, us Duncan's.

Permission, I sought, to see my parents.
Some weeks had passed since I last saw them.
A Saturday visit granted.
10:30am to 3:30pm.
Taking Baby Ruth with me.

My father, George,
around the campfire, shares with other Gunggari,
news from Mitchell Yumba.

Image of Yumba sign.

The yumba – a safe place to gather.
Yumba – Gunggari for 'home'.
The Yumba a place for Murri's.
Yumba – a community on the edge of town.
Aboriginal families drifting,
unable to find a place in Mitchell,
because of the colour of their skin.

The Yumba, where my father and mother met.
Married there, tribal way with Elders blessings.
Gunggari people were safe at the Yumba.
Houses, a school and a church.
The Yumba – East Mitchell Aboriginal Settlement.

But my parents shelter now,
in the Bottom Camp of Barambah,
where most of the Gungarri camp.

Pause.

My father is changing.

His earlier decision,
'... for just a little while'.

Ruby shakes her head with despair.

Being the devoted and obedient daughter,
challenging my father, I'd never done.
But couldn't he see this decision was wrong for his
family?
But they look happy: a Yumba, other Gunggari.
Employed – a man's pride.
Weekly rations.
Boys educated – although not heard from or seen ...

Maybe my parents thought,
the Yumba they'd built,
they'll get their children back.

Pause.

My parents weren't leaving.
Not without their children.

Too much red tape.
Living permanently under the complete control of
the government.

'... we are here to stay,' I thought.

Scene 8

~ 1934 ~

Ruby, twenty-four years old.

RUBY: 1934.
           Four years have passed.
           Ruth wanting to be like the big girls.

           'She becomes big girl and able …'
           Comes back to haunt me.

           Monday 6th of March.
           I'm called to Matron.

           'I'm sending Ruth to school.'

           'She too young, she's only four and a half!'
           I blurt. Talking out of turn.

           End of discussion.

           My daughter,
           my little girl,
           removed from my care.
           Big Girls quarters now.

           Four and a half years old.
           This new arrangement …
           lattice-work divide.
           Little Ruth can't come over to my side.
           Even though she knows I'm here.

Actor 1 becomes Little Ruthie, four and a half years old. She marches in, watching her mother sitting at the other end of the table.

LITTLE RUTHIE :

> At the long dinner table,
> I see my mum at every evening meal.
> Her attention I try to get.
> But my mum's face,
> it will not turn.

Little Ruthie deliberately drops spoons to the floor. Ruby resists to look. More spoons drop.

RUBY: Punishment was severe and swift.
                 I had to stand by and accept it.

                 Little Ruth was dealt with.

                 Cat-o'-nine-tails.

LITTLE RUTHIE:

> I'm 'big Girl now',
> I'm four and a half years old.

Beat.

RUBY: My torment is to get worse,
                 I'm now required to go out and work.

Image of Work Agreement.

RUBY: I have little time to be with Ruth.
                 The days going by, too fast.

Ruby joins Little Ruthie at the bed with her travel port (suitcase), they close it together.

> The day arrives; Ruth allowed to help pack my port.
> To stay with me until the taxi comes.
> With all the excitement that a taxi creates …
> A mother and daughter's hearts are breaking.
> Our second separation.

LITTLE RUTHIE:
> I'm five years old.

Little Ruthie exits.

Scene 9

Ruby is about twenty-six years old.

RUBY: My life now in the realm of domestic servitude.
         The people you work for take control of your life.
         I don't like it, but I do as I am told.
         Always obey.
         Always, the white man's way.
         You ask permission to do anything.
         Your wage, paid directly to Barambah Settlement.
         Pay your way.
         Living expenses.
         An allowance given.
         Surviving on pocket money.

Choreographed work routine repeated.

         Cooking.
         Cleaning.
         Caring for other children.
         The life, lonely.
         Your employers didn't form relations.
         Nobody socialised.

         My day started at the crack of dawn.
         Preparing wood fires.
         Cooking.
         Serving meals.
         Cleaning the large homes.
         Washing by hand.

39

At night.
I eat, alone.
A small room to sleep in.
'Look after yourself ... when that house is quiet.'

Ruby pushes the small dresser drawer in front of the door. Getting into bed.

Agonise over your life's direction.
Agonise over the loss of family connection.
Agonise ...

Curling onto the foetal position.

ACTOR 1:   Ruby illiterate, taught herself to crochet.
Quite adept, mastering complex patterns.

Actor 1 leaves her crochet (calico piece with crocheted edge) and becomes Little Ruthie reading a Boy's Own *book. Ruby gets out of bed. As she folds the blanket back to represent a new place, she is speaking her lines below.*

RUBY: First posting,
Cinnabar, 20 miles from Barambah.
The McGills.
I did extra work, cash in hand, mustering.
Skilled horsewoman.

Image of Ruby with her favourite horse.

My favourite horse called Shanghai.

Walking and talking, Ruby goes to the armchair and takes up the crocheting.

> Ruth was allowed to visit.
> Two weeks each Christmas.
> Discovered she loved to read.
> I didn't know how.
> Ruth and my secret.
> She's six and a half.
> Ruth teaches me to write.

Ruthie teaches her mother to write her name.

RUTHIE: 'R – straight up, curve around and kick it out.
               U – start there and bring it down and around and
               back up.'

RUBY: 'Like a smile.'

RUTHIE: 'We allowed to smile here.'

Beat.

RUBY: 'What letter is next?'

RUTHIE: 'B – like a loaf of bread.
               Or bum cheeks.'

Ruthie giggles, but it's short-lived.

RUBY: 'Ruthie, don't talk like that!'

RUTHIE: 'Y'

RUBY: 'Because if Mrs McGill hears you …'

RUTHIE: 'I mean the next letter, Y.'

RUBY: 'Oh.'

RUTHIE: 'Y – like that smile letter, U,
             but comes to a point at the bottom,
             with a tail.'

RUBY: 'Wow, look at that.
             That's my name.'

Ruthie nods.

RUBY: 'Ruby.'

Ruby admires their efforts. Memory holds.

RUTH: The McGill's were good people.
             They treated me like family.
             But it was Mum,
             didn't want me to be a part of their lives.
             She thought I was being disrespectful.
             But Mrs McGill encouraged me.
             Let me use the Rolo piano.
             I could play it anytime.
             Showed me her sons library books.
             Boy's Own collection.
             Read whenever I liked.

             But that kindness and acceptance was an exception,
             that I would never experience again.

Ruth becomes Little Ruthie again. With her back to her mother now, she continues reading.

RUBY: Ruth so independent.
              Us growing further apart.

              Next posting for me, the Barton's in Julia Creek.
              Then Mount Perry to work for the Briggs.
              Back to Cinnabar for another two years.

ACTOR 1: This scenario for Ruby
              was played out for the next fifteen years.
              Shunted from one place to another.
              performing domestic duties.
              A grown woman, thirty-four years old,
              still under the care and protection of 'The Act'.

              I'm fourteen.
              Entering my own work cycle.

Together they do a physical movement piece with a large piece of calico.

RUTH: Mother's last job in the district was Murgon,
              Comino's café.

BOTH: Three miles from each other.
              The closest we've been in years.

RUTH: I was told by others.

              'Ruby, in town.'

              I don't remember us connecting in this time …

for four months, before –

RUBY: I board a train to the big city.
         No more remote properties.
         Isolation on farms.
         I heard of the community forming.
         Brisbane Blacks.

         Time for change.
         Ruth, fourteen now, out working.
         She's gone from me to the system.
         Times are changing … a little for me.

Scene 10

~ 1944 ~

Ruby is around thirty-three years old. Actor 1 becomes Ranald Simmonds, a photographer who Ruby works for. He shows Ruby the portrait he took of her.

RANALD SIMMONDS:
       'Ruby? Ruby.'

RUBY: Ranald Simmonds,
       Professional photographer, Indooroopilly.

RANALD SIMMONS:
       'Ruby, look.'

Ranald is proud of his portrait of Ruby. She takes the photograph from him. Image of Ruby portrait is projected.

RANALD SIMMONS:
       'I've captured something there. Behind your eyes?'

RUBY: I see, her … not sure, who she is.
       I see …
       I'm not Ruth's mother …
       I'm not Frank's betrothed …
       I'm not me anymore, maybe I don't want to …
       see me …
       defeated, disheartened, detached …

       'Mr Simmonds, can you call me, Ruby Anne?
       Please?'

RANALD SIMMONDS:
            'Ruby? Are you … (all right).'

RUBY: 'Ruby Anne, please.'
            This is nice … thank you.'

She hands the photograph back to him, and he exits.

            But *this* Ruby Anne, got moxie!
            Back to Cherbourg for a visit.
            But Ruth, out working.
            Superintendent Semple still there.
            I'm talkin' up for the older inmates now.

            I ask:
            'Where's old Yellow Annie's son's war wages?'
            She didn't know sixpence from a shilling.
            Semple said,

            'What would you know?'

            And ordered me out of his office.
            Told them black policemen –

            'Get Ruby Duncan out of here.'

            Ooh, he didn't like me.
            Cheekiest gin on the Mission!

She laughs.

            Working in Brisbane had its advantage.
            On my days off, other Aborigines.

Brisbane Blacks.
Friendships formed.
To ease my pain and provide some fun.
Loved dancing at the Caledonian club.

Caledonian club music plays – Ruby and her friend, Rita (Actor 1), greet each other and dance.

RUBY: We talked about Country.

               'Rita, any news?'

               We hungered for.

RITA: 'Frank married another.
               Two years after you left.'

RUBY: 'Who?'

RITA: 'Gunggari. One of your friends. Judy.'

RUBY: 'Judy? Whom I told of Frank and me?
               Judy?! Who I shared my baby girl with!
               Judy?!! There when I'd visit Frank's family!!
               Judy!!!'

RITA: 'Ruby Anne, can we just dance.'

The women dance. Rita (Actor 1) steps away. Ruby dances, aggressively.

Ruth (actor 1) now back in 2004 – seventy-five years old, she holds the actual portrait of Ruby Anne.

RUTH: Ruby Anne.
          Now I understand mother's change of name.
          She was leaving her past behind.
          Which included me.

The moment fades away. Ruth exits.

Scene 11

~ 1947 ~

Ruby is in her mid-thirties. Images of Brisbane city life.

RUBY: I worked twenty years under the provisions of 'The Act'.
Receiving only pocket money.
Not given my passbook to check deposits, or withdrawals.

The control, debilitating.
Kept people on a leash.
No possibilities to dream or make plans.

Image of Exemption certificate projected.

Exemption 14th October 1947.
Certificate number 88/47.

My first act of freedom –
since my internment in the Women's dormitory,
Barambah, 1930,
– to receive my savings account balance,
kept since 1935.
My expectation – I'm rich!

Image of her savings account showing.

Twelve pounds, nine shillings and nine pence …
… for seventeen years of work.

Short-changed,
my life,
again!

My mind goes to Ruth.
Worried, for what she'll find in her future.

Beat.

Government curfews. Blacks out by Sundown.
Brisbane city boundaries established.
Boundary Street.
West End and Spring Hill.

I kept to the rules.
Business done.
Get on the bus.
Out of the city before curfew.
But Rita was late this day.
Comes dawdling my way.
I told her, 'Rita, don't be late.'
Anxious, on edge. I shape up.
She says, 'Wait there, Dunk, let me take my
Steppings off.'

She mimes taking of her slimming undergarments.

Tucks them under her arm.
Fist cocked ready to fly … when
the bus arrives.

House of employment,
not a minute late.

A call to the department, reported.

ACTOR 1:   Employers submitted reports.
           While the government assessed Ruby's application to
           be exempt.
           The comments read:

*Physical movement – Ruby is a puppet with a fake plastered smile,
being the obedient and obliging, happy Black. It's childlike.*

           "Ruby is happy."
           "Ruby is a nice bright girl."
           "Ruby is content."
           (*x4 repeat*)

BOTH: Ruby's thirty-seven.

Beat.

RUBY: Not wanting to be left on the shelf,
           I want to be married,
           a woman in my mid-thirties now.

           In 1947, I intend to marry.
           I had to report, still a ward of the state.

           On 8th of August, the department advised by phone:

Seventy-five-year-old Ruth, 2004, reads the file on her mother.

RUTH: '… the girl Ruby,
           was unwilling to sign a new agreement,
           to continue "in service".'

51

RUBY: So, my application for marriage denied.

Image of this letter is projected.

> He, a man of low character,
> they said.
> Then used the power of my request for exemption,
> against me.

RUTH: She had to, *break her association*.

RUBY: The threat was real,
and I complied.
Again.
I'm denied.
No future with my intended.

But, finally, freed from The Act,
October 1947.
But what is true freedom,
in a place that does not see you as equal?

I am Ruby Anne Duncan.
I possess a strong work ethic and excellent cooking
skills.
I will not let my illiteracy hold me back.

I rent a room at the Salvation Army Home, South
Brisbane.
And for the next ten years,
I worked in various places.
Heron Island.
Brisbane Girls Grammar School.

Northgate Hostel – house parent.
And from 1946 to 52, a domestic for –
Premier of Queensland, Mr Hanlon.
Never giving up on marriage,
at forty-six years old,
I meet Lenny Ray.
Taxi driver.
White fella, ten years younger.

Projected – image of a very happy Lenny and Ruby, arm in arm.

And twenty years after we met, we marry.

ACTOR 1:   She was sixty-six.
Her wedding ring her prize possession.

RUBY: Mrs Ruby Anne Ray.

Image dissolves and lights fade on Ruby.

PART III
Ruth

Scene 12

~ 1996 ~

Ruth aged sixty-six in 1996, back in her chair.

RUTH: By the time Mum started her journey back to me,
we were strangers.
Relationship strained.
Our closeness … there was none.
The damage, done.

By the time Mum started her journey back to me,
I was a grown woman.
Married with children.
I was not her good girl.
A disappointment.
My oldest two daughters,
out of wedlock.
Two different fathers.
Freedom came at a price.
We learned by trial and error.
The shameful return to Barambah Mission,
pregnant.
Interrogated.
Ruby angry.
No contact.
Deepening the rift of mother and daughter.

Ruby didn't approve of my marriage to a 'Camp
Boy,'
my childhood sweetheart – Joe.

But in time her anger and disappointment did go.
I did become Ruby's 'good girl'.
Respected member of the AIM church,
recognised community member,
numerous accolades and awards.

A mature Ruby appears, aged forty-six.

We're both willin' to try now, Christmas 1957.
Ruby is forty-six.
I'm twenty-seven.
She, acceptin' of my husband,
because of our love for my children.
Five at this stage.
Eight in total.
Cassandra, Glenys, Norman, adopted daughter,
Pheonia – Joe's youngest sister's girl.
Then, Mayleah, Duncan, Moira and Emmanuel.

Mother and I becoming close again.
Through her need and desire to share.
My excuse to ask her questions.

'Mum, I wanna write a book.'

I had always wanted to write a book.
I thought about it many times.
But doubt would take over.
My limited education.
I didn't have the time.
Convincin' myself,
I'd do it later,
when the time was right.

I guess, it's right.

The two women sit.

Now two mature women.
Both mothers, relivin' our past.
Talkin' about painful times.
We hadn't really discussed before.

(*Aside*) I ask her ...

RUTH: 'What were you feelin' at the time of our separation?'
           (*Aside*) Not waiting for her reply ...

           'I waited and waited by the lattice-work divide.
           Tryin' to catch a glimpse of you,
           but you didn't come.'

RUBY: 'You remember that?'

Ruth can only nod.

           'We're opening a chapter of our lives,
           that has remained closed,
           for a good many years, Ruth.'

RUTH: I think she was hopin' it would remain closed ...

Pause.

RUBY: 'I knew you were there.
           It was better you didn't see me.'

RUTH: (*Aside*) I wasn't ready to surrender and let go.

'That first night without you, I cried and cried.
I wanted to call out,
"Good night, Mum!"
in my loudest voice.

I would steal glimpses of you when I walked past the
sewing room.
I thought how pretty you were.
You're long jet-black hair,
always worn in braids,
neatly twisted in buns over each ear.
Or when you sat at the table,
across the same dining room.
Girls on one side,
the women on the other.
We ate in complete silence.
Oh, how I wanted to yell,
"Good morning, Mum!"
in my loudest voice.
"How are you this morning, Mum?"
I didn't though.

Neither did you, nor could you, call out to me.'

Both women quite stoic.

BOTH: We are not allowed to cry.
Crying always results in punishment.
We don't cry.

Memory – Actor 1 and Actor 2 join in with the voiceover of the Young Female Voices teasing.

YOUNG FEMALE VOICES (VO):
>'Cry-baby bunting, mother went a hunting.'

LITTLE RUTHIE:
>(*Internal thought*) Runnin' home from school …
>I spot you … waitin' for me.

RUBY: (*To audience*) Mothers tried to stay out of sight,
>not to upset the children.

LITTLE RUTHIE:
>(*Internal thought*) There had to be somethin' wrong.
>The other kids yelled,
>'Hey, Ruthie, ya mum's waitin' for ya.'
>
>I slow.
>(*Internal thought*) Mothers did not wait for their
>little girls at the dormitory.
>To find her waitin' for me made me feel …
>very nervous.
>
>I hadn't been this close to her,
>in what seemed like a long, long … long time.

Ruth steps up to Ruby. Playing the expectation, they might hug.

RUBY: 'Ruth, wajana [wa-jah-nah] ngija [Nigh-ah].
>[I am going away.]
>Gura [Goor-rah] ngiya [Nigh-ah] gandala
>[Gun dah-lah].

[I will come back.]'

LITTLE RUTHIE:
> (*Internal thought*) I really didn't know what that
> meant.

RUBY: 'Ruth, I'm being sent out to work.
> You won't see me for a while.
> Bigarringa [Bigga-reena] ngiya [nigh-ah] yindala
> [yin-darla].'
> [I will dream of you.]

LITTLE RUTHIE:
> (*Internal thought*) What's she sayin'?

RUBY: 'I will dream of you.'

The Young Female Voices (VO) – 'Cry-baby Bunting' is heard again.
Ruthie goes to hug her mother. Ruby steps away.

RUBY: (*Internal thought*) What could I do to let Ruth know
> I love her?
> That I care.
>
> In my work agreement,
> between the Barambah Settlement and employer –
>
> '… Ruth can draw from my account …
> two shillings a fortnight.
> … And … a standing order at the Murgon Bakery,
> a birthday cake … every birthday, until Ruth is
> fourteen.
> Please?'

Ruby slowly retreats – their goodbye. Ruth swings between older Ruth remembering but re-enacting as Little Ruthie.

RUTH: (*To audience*) Leading up to Mother's departure,
          (*Re-enact*) I sit at the lattice-work divide,
          face pressed firmly against it,
          watching, in case I missed her leavin'.

          (*To audience*) Not sure if we'd get to say goodbye.
          Even when ordered to bed,
          (*Re-enact*) I'd sneak back,
          only to run back inside.
          'Is that you, Ruthie?'

          All that is said.

          I was not lookin' forward to that day, but it came.
          I helped pack Mum's port.
          Waited with Mum until the taxi came.
          There was great excitement when the taxi arrived.
          Any vehicle pullin' up in front of the dormitory
          caused excitement.
          I tried to enter in the fun.
          We made our goodbyes without too much fuss.
          And then she was gone.

          This, our second separation.

I was surrounded by all the other kids.
There was nowhere to go and hide, to cry.
No place I could be alone.

With all this emotion locked inside my young body,
it's no wonder, I become, one of the naughtiest kids!
Not the only naughty kid,
because we all suffered,
the trauma of separation.

Scene 13

~ 1935 ~

Image of girls praying. Actor 2 is one of the older female inmates now. Ruthie is five years old. There are voices of the many young female inmates in this prayer. The actors join in with the voiceover.

INMATES: '… And lead us not into temptation but deliver us from evil. For thine is the Kingdom, forever and ever. Amen.'

They sing. Little Ruth joins in.

INMATES: 'Now the day is over, night is drawing nigh. Shadows of the evening, spill across the sky.'

Ruth becomes dominant.

LITTLE RUTHIE:
'Da da da da da da da da da da,
Four and twenty black birds baked in a pie …'

I didn't know the words.
I made them up as I went.
And tonight, I DIDN'T CARE!

Actor 2 takes the role of the House Parent/Old Granny.

HOUSE PARENT/OLD GRANNY:
'Is that you, Ruthie? Come out here!'

Beat.

LITTLE RUTHIE:

I walk out onto the veranda.

HOUSE PARENT/OLD GRANNY:

'Kneel on the floor.'

Little Ruthie does.

HOUSE PARENT/OLD GRANNY:

'How dare you do that to the Lord's prayer.'

LITTLE RUTHIE:

I kneel until everyone is asleep.

The lights fade to only the lantern light, flickering on stage again. And the night sounds take over.

RUTH: I was feeling bad enough.
          I just said goodbye to my mum.
          No idea when I was to see her again, if ever.
          I was lectured about hell.
          Told I'd end up there if I didn't behave.

          This was the first night of a long string of
          punishments.

House Parent/Old Granny appears as an ominous shadow in the doorway.

HOUSE PARENT/ OLD GRANNY:

'Is that you, Ruthie? You better settle down.'
'Is that you, Ruthie? I'll come in there to you soon.'

RUTH: I was to hear those words, 'Is that you, Ruthie?' many times, more.

Night sounds grow as the lantern flickers out.

Scene 14

~ 1943 ~

New day. Ruthie now a teenager. Actor 2 will play teenage Marcia.

RUTHIE: '(*Whispering*) Marcia, come on.'

Teenage Ruthie tiptoeing. Marcia falls in beside Ruthie. Ruthie in the voice of the House Parent.

       'Is that you, Ruthie?'

The girls freeze.

       (*More authority*) 'Is that you Ruthie?'

MARCIA: 'Yes, it is.'

RUTHIE: I could have killed Marcia.
             Even if she is my very best friend.

They play-push each other.

MARCIA: Teenagers now, a little more freedom.
             A lot more chores to do, but freedom.
             We didn't need supervision to play down at the duck pond.

BOTH: Saturday – duck pond day!

RUTHIE: At the end of the school week, always on my best behaviour.

Choreographed stylised work routine adapted and repeated.

> I didn't want to miss out on my one magical day
> of fun.
> By ten-thirty, works done!

BOTH: 'Saturday – duck pond day!'

Physical – Running routine.

RUTHIE: This is freedom time.
            An all-day adventure.

MARCIA: A day out for the big girls!

            'Come on, Ruthie!'

RUTHIE: 'I'm comin', Marcia!'

Physicalisation.

MARCIA: Out the dormitory yard.

RUTHIE: Through the back gate,
            out past the lavatory block.

BOTH: Phew!

RUTHIE: Drums of goona!
            (*Aside*) Collected, Mondays.

MARCIA: Pass the school, and down near the creek.

They sing and dance to the original song, 'Hail, Hail the Gangs all here.' With voiceover of the many young female inmates joining in.

BOTH: Hail, hail, the gang's all here.
                 We're a bunch of live ones, not a single dead one.
                 Hail, hail, the gang's all here.
                 Sure, I'm glad that I'm here too!
                 Hail, hail, the gang's all here,
                 never mind the weather, here we are together!
                 Hail, hail, the gang's all here.
                 Sure, we're glad that you're here, too!

RUTHIE: There was Loysee, Bethal, Nell, Dell,
                 Evelyn, Elsie, Elvie, Viola, Violet, Wilma.

MARCIA: Me – Marcia,
                 Enid, Jean, Doreen,
                 Myra, Martha, Marsha,
                 Peggy, Penny, Pearl and Faith.

RUTHIE: Grace, Gladys, Gale.
                 Jean S, Helen, Rachel, and me – Ruthie.
                 All us big girls!

BOTH: Dommo Girls!

MARCIA: Scramblin' through the last barbed-wire fence,
                 a transformation takes place.

RUTHIE: I was no longer Ruthie,
                 I was Alice – Alice Faye – my favourite movie star.

Four images appear of Alice Faye, and Ruthie strikes the matching poses.

MARCIA: I was Betty Grable, pin-up girl.

Four images appear of Betty Grable, and Marcia strikes the matching poses. Then one repeat of the actors doing their poses together.

BOTH: We all had one.

They laugh.

MARCIA: Martha was Ginger Rodgers.
She saw the film, 'Top Hat',
at the Barambah Hall,
picture night,
once a month … 'but not for all'.

RUTHIE: 'Shut up, Marcia.'
Martha thought, she could tap dance.

MARCIA: Tin lids strapped to her toes!

Movie image of 'Top Hat' dance routine. Marcia does a very bad and funny tap dance routine. Using the spoons as the tapping sound, the faster Ruthie taps the spoons, the faster and clumsier the tap dance gets.

MARCIA: (*Frustrated*) Knock it off, Ruthie!

The girls collapse into each other, laughing.

MARCIA: Marsha was Paulette Goddard. In the movies that lady smoked long cigarettes.

RUTHIE: We'd all imitate her.

MARCIA: Found a tree with porous roots.

RUTHIE: We'd dig them out.

MARCIA: Cut them to cigarette size.

RUTHIE: And we light them!

The girls draw back on their pretend long smokes and start coughing on pretend smoke.

MARCIA: You never inhale.

RUTHIE: Burnt throats.

They laugh again.

RUTHIE: Our fantasies helped us to cope.
            The duck pond now a lagoon from the film, *South of Pago Pago*. 1940 – Action/adventure/romance.

Image of the poster for the film, 'South of Pago Pago'. A moment in the film, where the man chases, the native girl is play-acted out, it's fun and light, matching the heroic embrace on the poster.

            In reality,
            the duck pond was weedy.
            Water green.
            It stank.
            Lots of rubbish.

MARCIA: No swimming or drinking.

RUTHIE: No romantic chase and dive scene!

MARCIA: No, but this was our …

BOTH: Shangri-la!

MARCIA: Where movies are acted out.

RUTHIE: And dreams come true.

The music of 'By a Waterfall' begins, and Marcia and Ruthie dance the Kaleidoscope Water routine, from the film, Footlight Parade. *An image of this Kaleidoscope Water routine is projected.*

RUTHIE: Old Granny was so impressed.
            She asked Matron if we could dance, regularly,
            at the community hall dance night.

MARCIA: Three performances we did.
            Barefoot, in our calico nightdresses.

RUTHIE: We thought we were great,
            until one of them bloomin' Camp Boys
            booed us. Right off stage!

Seated back up on the top ramp landing.

MARCIA: (*Aside*) Speaking of –
            'Hey, Ruthie, look who's there?'

RUTHIE: 'Shut up, Marcia.'

Image of young Joe Hegarty appears.

> Me, eyes only for my Camp Boy, Joe.

Marcia makes a face, not impressed with loved-up Ruthie.

RUTHIE: The camp kids, mission mob,
                considered wayward, no good.
                Didn't have the discipline of the Dormitory.

MARCIA: We'd wait for them on the log that had fallen across
                the creek.
                'What did you Camp Boys bring us today?'
                Gifts of small wild birds,
                already plucked and cleaned.

RUTHIE: These, we'd mix with vegetable peels, dug out of
                bins.

MARCIA: Cooked in a jam tin.
                These ingredients,
                with a pinch of salt,
                made a delicious stew.

                'Ruthie, salt.'

Ruthie checks her pockets.

MARCIA: 'Don't muck-around. Salt.'

RUTHIE: 'We forgot the salt.'

MARCIA: 'You forgot the salt.'

RUTHIE: No one wanted to go back for it.

MARCIA: If one of the grown-ups saw you, they'd be sure to find you a job.

Scene 15

~ 1943 ~

Through this scene the actors take turns in voicing the House Parent/ Old Granny.

The two girls are sneaking along the Dormitory veranda, hoping not to be heard by the House Parent/Old Granny.

MARCIA: So, we're sneaking along the veranda, all for bloomin' salt.

                'Who's that? Is that you, Ruthie?'

RUTHIE: She had hearin' like them camp dogs.

MARCIA: She could bristle to.

RUTHIE: Sharp as a tack, Old Granny.

BOTH: We stood holdin' our breath.

They indicate to each other to be still and quiet. Ruthie voices House Parent/Old Granny.

RUTHIE: '(*More authority*) Is that you, Ruthie?'

MARCIA: Demanding an answer.
           'Yes, it is.'

RUTHIE: I could have killed Marcia!
           'I'm coming!' I say, as obedient as ever.'

I slowly walk in, and there they are.
Four old ladies playin' euchre.

I knew, I was in for it.

Ruthie rubs her bottom preparing for the strap.

But … there, in front of Old Granny, was the half
dolly peg.

*Actor 2 becomes the House Parent/Old Granny, handing Ruthie the
half dolly peg.*

HOUSE PARENT/OLD GRANNY:
    'Here.'

RUTHIE: She said.

HOUSE PARENT/OLD GRANNY:
    'Crack this in my head.'

RUTHIE: She thought she had munyoos [mŏŏn-youse], nits.
    Her hair grey, almost white, and short.
    There was a mass of it.
    Probably very curly when she was young.
    A handsome woman.
    She had no munyoos.
    But the peg treatment, relaxing.

Action of hair treatment with peg.

A few of us had been caught before.
We had a plan.

A small pinch of sugar sprinkled in her hair was all
it took.
The sugar, when crack between thumbnail and peg,
made noise like a nit cracking,

The actor demonstrates.

… giving this old girl, satisfaction.

HOUSE PARENT/ OLD GRANNY:
'Ooooh, that's gooood.'

Actor 2:   Ruthie was not looking forward to the next stage of
her life –
going out to work. She'd turned fourteen.
Marcia and Ruthie, the only two left from their old
gang.
Loysee, Peg, Jean, Enid, Marsha, Bethel and Doreen
had all gone out.
Faith and Pearl had early marriages.
Martha was also off.
Tore their hearts out to see them go.
For the ten previous years they'd moved as a team.
Fighting the 'Camp Girls'.
Battling the system.
Surviving.
'The Act' – the care and the protection you could
only call barbaric.
Not even knowing why they were there.

Ruth, aged sixty-six in 1996, sitting back in her armchair.

RUTH: I'm not aware that anyone had ever told us why we
           were there.
           Some may argue we got looked after.
           We were fed, clothed and had a roof over our head.
           But was that enough?
           Would that be enough for your children?
           Could this system ever take your place as the loving
           caring parent?
           Would you let it?
           Ruby had to pretend in her heart,
           this place, the dormitory, was best for me.

She asks the audience.

           Could you?
           Would you?

           But the separation of mother and daughter
           was nowhere near as painful now.
           The Dormitory was home,
           with all its rules and regulations.
           I had conformed.
           Succumbed to its formalities.
           Why fight it?
           I couldn't.
           A ward of the State.
           Neglected … so they said.

PART IV
Ruthie to Work

Scene 16

~ 1944 ~

Images of kids being schooled. Sir Leslie Orme Wilson, Governor of Queensland from 1932–1946, gives a speech.

Governor (VO): 'It seems far more important to me; that Aboriginal children should be instructed in practical work [that is labour and servants] than in history or geography. Once they learn to read and write and do simple arithmetic, that would seem all that is required.'

Ruthie (Actor 1) grabs her travel port (suitcase).

RUTHIE: 1944.
                Fourteen now.
                Finally, the day had come.
                We all knew it would happen.
                You just *left* the day after your birthday.
                No matter of where it fell throughout the year.
                No-one was ever ready.
                To Matron Pascoe,
                just as Mother had done.
                'Please' I said to myself, 'Don't send me today.'
                A lecture on how to conduct myself.
                Then, off to the store.
                My order, it was standard for every girl sent out.
                I owned nothing of a personal nature.

Reads from inventory:
                • 1 suitcase
                • 1 hat
                • 2 panties

- 1 towel
- 2 house dresses
- 1 nightdress
- 1 good dress
- 1 nightgown
- 1 cardigan
- 1 pair of shoes
- 1 comb
- 1 pair of slippers
- new issue of sanitary napkins and belt
- 1 pair of stockings
- 1 suspender belt
- toothpaste and brush
- A bar of Lux soap ...

Ruthie smells it. It's scented.

Scented soap! First time, for anyone!
Wonder how much this is goin' to cost me?!
None of this is free.
Paid it back from our very low wages.

Travel arrangements are made.
A place I'd never heard of.
Jandowae.
The time to depart is set.

Last day in the dormitory, I'm really scared.
On my own, my first big trip.
This was to be my greatest test.

I pass the well-groomed garden,
the six-foot barbed-wire fence,

thorny roses creep over it.
A look back to the dormitory,
in all its frightful authority and glory …

All the kids out front
to wave goodbye and chase the taxi down the road.

I look at all their faces.
I wonder if I'd ever see them again.
There, in the crowd, my sweetheart, my Camp Boy,
Joe.

It was a sad Little Ruthie getting' on the train.
The railway carriage,
the big black shiny seat,
my feet barely touch the floor.
All the passengers, white.
No one speaks to me.
So scared travellin' at night.
Lots of questions runnin' through my head.
I try to sleep.
Hungry.
The loneliness, I cannot describe.

I think of the dormitory,
surrounded by the girls.
So many years under a watchful adult eye.
Not daring to make a move without permission.
Weren't used to actin' alone.
The older women's advice came back to me.

'Be as though you aren't there.
Fade into the background.'

The train stops.
I hear the station master cry –
a name that kind of sounded like, Jandowae.
With port in hand, the door will not open.
I hear the whistle. I panic.
The train lurches forth.
I stumble.
Out.
Train moves off.

Actor 2 enters stage as the Station Master.

STATION MASTER:
'Tickets!'

RUTHIE: He looks at it and he says,

STATION MASTER:
'Girlie, you got off at the wrong station!
Where are you goin'?'

She hands the Station Master a letter.

RUTHIE: This letter was carried by every Aboriginal
that left the mission for outside employment.
Introducing me and my destination.
And to whom I was to go to.

He shakes his head.
Indicating, to sit on the long seat outside.

STATION MASTER:
'The rail motor will be through in the mornin'.'

RUTHIE: I'm left alone,
          to wait,
          the whole night,
          on a dark platform.

          The sounds of the night echo around me.
          Hungry, alone, and … I need to 'go'.

          'Can't pee on the grass.
          I'll be caught and punished.'

          Mornin', stomach, bloated.
          The station door opened
          to the Ladies, what a relief!

Scene 17

~ 1943 ~

The Boss's Son (Actor 2), Ruthie's new employer enters.

BOSS'S SON:
    'You're late.'

RUTHIE: Said the Boss's son, there to meet me.

BOSS'S SON:
    'Ya shoulda bin'ere yesta'dee.'

RUTHIE: That was our introduction.
    I never like him from that day.

    The Mistress, his mother, was as short as I.
    Seventy years old, with a no-nonsense face.
    The Boss, her husband, as tall as she was short.
    Two sons, Mr Jack and Mr Dick.
    My first impression, nothin' had changed.
    The Mistress, the matron.
    The old man, the Boss.
    And the sons, well,
    like all white officials,
    untouchables.

    I knew my place, immediately.
    Put down.
    Servant to master.
    Be silent and obey.

(*Aside*) Can you imagine, me, bein' silent?
After the cold reception,
taken to my room.
It was as small as it was bare.
A bed, wardrobe and dressing table.
An emptiness.
A deadness.
No warmth of my Dommo Girls.
I'm missin' their voices.

I'm called to lunch,
a place set at the kitchen table.
The food a welcoming sight.
I hadn't eaten for nearly twenty-four hours.
Being a dormitory girl, you never complained.
You accept your fate in silence.

I did try, my best, not to object.

After lunch, I was allowed time to myself
and glad when night fell.

I imagined many things that first night.
Alone, for the first time in my life.
And I was very, very frightened.

Before going to sleep
I remembered what the old women told me ...

Ruthie pushes the small dressing table in front of the door. She gets into bed.

It was only then,

could I close my eyes,
and finally drift off to sleep.

One thing for certain,
if I followed the rules,
and did the work the best I could,
I would go home to the dormitory a changed person.
No longer a child in the girl's ward,
I'd be comin' home,
to a bed, on the *women's side* of the dormitory.
This is important to me.
It was the rule,
that if you signed a twelve-month contract and
it was not honoured,
you could do punishment.
And add insult to injury,
you would have to stay in the little girl's ward at the
dormitory.
Or even worse, sent to Palm Island – penal colony.
Never to return.

I hadn't heard of anyone,
who had *not*
completed their first twelve months of work.

… I did try my best.

Repeat choreographed cleaning routine.

My routine:
Make my bed.
Make the mornin' fire –
paper, kindling, wood stove.

Prepare breakfast.
Set the table, serve breakfast.
Take my own breakfast.

Then, clean their bed pots –
on a full stomach, mind you –
that was punishment enough.
Prepare morning tea.
Serve morning tea.
Take my own morning tea.
On and on it went until the instructions finished
at 3pm.
I had never ever worked that hard in my short life.
An hour's rest and back at it again.
Afternoon tea.
Prepare and serve dinner.
I could not go to bed
until all the fire and heat were gone out of the stove,
to be set for the following mornin',
with paper, kindling, wood.
Every day this routine went on.

Well into my twelve-month contract, now.

A re-enactment of being paid by the Mistress (Actor 2).

On Fridays, with all the pomp and ceremony
of a big corporate chief,
The Mistress came armed
with my pocketbook, and pen.

Mistress holds open the pocketbook and offers the pen.

MISTRESS: 'Do you write?'

RUTHIE: 'Very well. Thank you.'

Ruthie signs and Mistress hands over the money.

>Two shillings and sixpence,
>my pocket money.
>The other two and six,
>sent back to a 'bank account',
>Cherbourg Mission.
>Savings.
>I could be rich.

>I want to save my two and six for a new dress.

Ruthie goes to her room with the notepad and pen.

>When I wasn't working,
>I was in my room writing.
>I loved to write:
>to Marica,
>to my other Dommo Sisters,
>even to the little girls still there.
>To Mother.

MISTRESS: 'You're wasting your time!'

RUTHIE: I wasn't about to be told what I should do in my
            time off.

>'Don't treat me like a servant.'

I left the dormitory intending to have some freedom.

MISTRESS: 'Do you know who you are talking to?'

RUTHIE: 'I will not bow down.
I will not be walked over.'

I was always very good at standin' up for my rights.

MISTRESS: 'You insolent and cheeky girl! How dare you!'

RUTHIE: Maybe I said too much …
out loud.

I was punished.
But no cat-o'-nine-tails.
No kneeling until the lantern burns dry.

But because of my contract,
I was to go everywhere the Mistress went.
Every Friday night we went to the pictures.
Before my outburst, the Mistress paid my way.

Remember, I wanted my savings for my new dress.
Remember, my savings were two shillings and
sixpence.
The Mistress's punishment – me, to pay my own way
to the pictures.
And yes, the tickets were … two and six!

Very soon, I began to feel the effects
of not having any money to spend at all.

It was difficult to write any letters as I had little
writing paper.
I couldn't purchase toiletries.
Rather than go to Mistress,
I write a letter to Mother.
Remember, Mother had trouble reading and writing.

Ruthie writes the letter. Actor 2 enters as Ruby, thirty-three years old.

RUBY: I got my Mistress to read the letter to me.

RUTHIE: '... everyone is good to me, all except the Mistress
             and her sons. She's got an absent mind; she always
             thinks bad of me.
             She said I have a big bum. I don't take any notice of her.
             It goes in one ear and out the other. She's like a big
             baby,
             always poking faces at me.'

RUBY: I'm not sure how to react.
             My Mistress shocked,
             and told me as Ruth's mother,
             I should speak my mind.

             'Speak my mind?'
             Easy said than done.

             I was afraid I'd be punished, sent to Palm Island.
             But she reassured me, she'd speak for me.

RUTHIE: My Mistress received a letter from the
             Superintendent,
             29th of May 1944.

94

Image of the letter projected.

RUTHIE: Dear Madame,

Re: Ruth Duncan

The mother of the above-named ... has approached me
to *increase this girl's pocket money.*
I am agreeing with her request and Agreement
22725 is being varied to provide for payment of
pocket money 5 shillings per week, and credit Saving
Bank Account here 7 and 6 per week from the 1st of
July next ...

How about that!
A win for me!
I didn't ask for a raise.
(*tongue in cheek*) Compensation?
And of course, the battle went on.

MISTRESS: 'Ruth! You hopeless, untrained—'

RUTHIE: Trying to break my spirit.

MISTRESS: '—uneducated, impertinent ... riffraff.'

Beat.

RUTH: Twelve months at that job, transformed me.
I'm no longer the frightened girl,
who waved goodbye to her friends,
as the taxi drove through the front gate of the Mission.
Going through that gate into a world unknown,

I realised, I was important too.
For all my life in the dormitory,
treated by those in charge as someone who had no
feelings. Simply trained to obey.
Not a creature made of flesh and blood.
Never regarded as someone's daughter.
A living human being who had needs and dreams.
The words:
Is. That. You. Ruthie.

Echoes around the space.

So that, having my named called,
held no endearment,
just a threat of punishment.
Cannot be removed or forgotten!

Beat.

I left that workplace with an awareness
that I had rights.
That objecting to how I was treated,
writing letters to the authorities,
could have positive results.
I'm twenty-one. And empowered.

PART V
Ruth and Ruby

Scene 18

~ 1951 ~

Ruthie, draped in calico, while an inmate (Actor 2) makes adjustments to her (calico material) wedding dress.

INMATE: 'You're out of the system now, Ruthie.
                Marrying your Joe. Lucky you.
                Is your mother coming?
                To the wedding?"

Ruthie shakes her head, no.

INMATE: 'Why not? She has exemption.'

RUTHIE: 'Yes, got it in 1947.
                Haven't seen hide nor hair, Sis.'

INMATE: 'Why wouldn't she come?'

RUTHIE: 'To be exempt … is to turn your back on your own.
                It's a must.
                You need permission to visit.
                Pay to stay.
                Lots of red tape, muckin' about.
                Superintendent final say, anyway.
                It's best this way …'

Ruthie stands in her (calico) wedding dress. The inmate becomes Ruby, forty years old.

RUBY: 1951.

I received word that my only daughter,
Ruth Elizabeth, who is now twenty-one,
is marrying a 'Camp Boy'.

RUTHIE: Mother made it very clear.

RUBY: I did not approve.

Image of Ruthie on her wedding day, and Uncle Eric Duncan giving her away. Wedding photo of Joe and Ruth.

Scene 19

Ruby, aged forty-six, sits on a chair. Ruthie, aged twenty-eight, holds a swaddled baby (the wedding calico wrap).

RUBY: It was the children that brought us back together.
By the time I started my journey back to my
daughter she had—

RUTHIE: My fifth child,
Duncan, 11th of December 1957,
Two weeks old.

Christmas dinner cemented our relationship.

RUBY: I accepted her husband, Joe.

RUTHIE: It was the children that brought us back together,
our shared love for them.
And Ruby Anne had finally found love
with Leonard Ray.

Image of Lenny and Ruby projected.

Taxi drive for Yellow Cabs.
White fella, and ten years younger.
She wanted to show him off.
But they loved each other.
And she wanted us to meet him.

We got a big shock,
when the Yellow cab,
pulls up at my mother-in-law's –
Cherbourg mission.
I think the whole street came to look.
My oldest children reckon,
'Someone rich comin' here, Mum.
Yellow cab, all the way from Brisbane.'
'Who do we know who's rich?'

Ruby talks to her grandchildren about culture. Ruthie watches intrigued.

RUBY: (*Telling the children*)
            'Maranoamundu [Mar-ra-no-a mun-do] ngalinda
            [narl-lyn-da].
            We are from the Maranoa.
            Gunggari ngalinda [Goong-gar-ree narl-lyn-da].
            We are Gunggari.
            Yumba yumbana [Yum-ba yum-ban-nah].
            "Yumba" is the word for home.'

RUTHIE: And I say,
            'You've known this all this time?'

            I believed that all I was,
            was a Dommo Girl who had no culture.
            No language. No Country.
            This was a total shock to me.
            It amazed me. Mother has language,
            after all these years.
            She and the other women in the dormitory,
            ordered not to use their language.

(*Smiling*) I'm thrilled …
'I want to know more.'

Ruby takes the swaddled baby from Ruthie. Ruby begins to sing to him. Ruthie watches from a distance, quietly sings, repeating the words after her mother.

RUBY: (*Singing*) Mar-ra warren no.
          I watch Ruth from the corner of my eye.
          (*Singing*) Mar-ra wothen no.
          Biyulbiwal [Bee-yul-bee-wal] mundane [mun-dun-a],
          give her the spirit of life.

          (*Singing*) Mar-ra wothen no.
          She's awoken.
          (*Singing*) Mar-ra warren no.
          As much as I sing for my grandchildren,
          I sing for my only daughter.
          For all the times I couldn't.

Beat.

RUTHIE: But I'm still angry with Mother.
          I need answers.

RUBY: And I knew Ruth harboured deep resentment
          towards me …

Scene 20

~ 1996 ~

Ruth is sixty-six years old. Ruby is eighty-six.

RUTH: It wasn't until Mother was eighty-six years old.
             Thirty-nine years later, after that first Christmas
             together,
             when I put pen to paper for the book,
             I try again.

             'Why did you leave me?'

Pause.

RUBY: When the other little girls
             that you played with
             were removed from their mothers,
             separated into the little girl's dorm,
             you would cry for them, Ruth.
             You'd watch them march off to school each day,
             but you were determined to be with them.
             You would sneak away from me –
             you only had to walk through the dormitory back
             gate.
             And your Uncle Glen, 'bout thirteen at the time,
             would have to bring you home.
             He growls, and say,

             'You wanna keep this kid home, Ruby, she make me
             shame.'

I very much wanted to keep you home,
but I couldn't watch you every hour.
I had to work toward our upkeep.
Matron made sure I knew how she felt, about you
sneaking off.
The tone of her voice terrified me.

'I'm sending Ruth to school.'

Matron took control of the situation
and decided what should be done.
And she did. End of discussion.

RUTHIE: Well, that's what happened then.
            It was me …

RUBY: No, Ruth.
            You were beside yourself.
            Excited to be going to school.
            I tried to share in the excitement with you.
            But this day had much more implication and hurt
            for me.
            I dressed you that morning.
            Royal Blue uniform, white blouse
            I'd sewn and pressed.
            Pinning a tiny handkerchief.
            You looked like every other child,
            waiting in line, to be checked by Matron.

            Your face beaming.
            My heart breaking.
            My little girl off to big school.
            Your first day was my last day as your mother.

I smiled at you. Off you marched.
You didn't see me wipe my tears away.

That afternoon when you came home,
you rushed to tell me of your day, then,
the reality hit in, hard.

You couldn't come over to the Mothers' side of the
dormitory,
it was forbidden.

I had to pretend in my heart
that this was the best for you.
All the while harbouring a heavy load of guilt.
You only wanting to share with me the joys of your
first day.

BOTH: Dormitory rules and regulations.
          Contact, forbidden.

          We had, 'The Act' – Care. Protection. Controlled.

*Image of Ruth and Ruby at the beach. Aunty Ruth voiceover having
the final word on 'The Act'.*

*Ruth Hegarty (VO): 'I'd call us prisoners, more or less, in that Home
– the dormitory. That, they just ... collected us for their own reasons
... never did care or protect us at all. But they didn't break our spirits.
Maybe they thought they did. But they did not break our spirits. We
were tough people.'*

Beat.

RUTH: Remember Marcia? Saturday – duck pond day!

Ruth goes back to her chair.

We were still livin' on the mission, at this time.
We had spoken this day.
Those talks, rare now
with children to care for,
husband's needs tendered to.
The struggles mission life threw at us,
under government control, still.
Her bruises on her face were not as visible, this day.
But I saw them. I knew where to look.
I knew how to hide mine.
I just didn't come out of my room.
His excuse,

'You're mine. You'll do as you're told!'
'You think you're better than the rest of us!'
'I own you!'

My husband discouraged
Marcia's and my friendship.
I had to be content with chance meetings
down at the Ration shed.
Collecting our weekly sugar, flour and tea.
A bit of meat if you were lucky.

It was comforting,
knowing Marcia was there, though.

It was hard not being able to share with her my
secret thoughts.

Maybe Joe didn't want us to compare.
Did that scare him?

Our kindred spirits,
our daring nature,
our forth righteousness,
us Dormitory Sisters.
Those Saturdays of freedom,
down at the duck pond,
our Shangri-la.

Maybe, Marcia and I,
would have done somethin',
about each other's predicament.

Memory – Actor 2 becomes pregnant Marcia.

RUTH: 'Marcia, you are as big as a house!
           How many is this one?'

MARCIA: 'Five.'

RUTH: I see she has a few new bruises.
           'Here, you want a smoke?'

MARCIA: 'Sorry, Sis, I'm a Christian now.
           I've given up the smokes.'

RUTH: I tease her, but she's serious.
           She appeared to have more courage about her.
           We talk for hours over mugs of tea.
           Mostly about how we weren't fitting into Camp life.

Where everyone's lifestyle and customs were different
to the life we left in the dormitory.

MARCIA: 'Ruthie, I might have to go.
This baby's sittin' low.'

RUTH: 'You look like you're ready to drop.'

The two friends embrace.

RUTH: And as she walked out my front gate,
I wondered when I would see her again.

Pause.

In childbirth that night, she died.
Her baby girl survived.

Her funeral procession passin'.
I stood back at a distance.
Unbelieving.
Gone to soon.

After her funeral.
I stood before her God and asked,
'Why? Why my best friend?'

I didn't think her God would be listening.
But amid my anger and grief,
Marcia's God touched my life that very night.
Her place in my heart, *He* took.
A Christian, I become.

I pay great tribute to my dear friend.
How bittersweet.

Marcia's death served to free me from my fears.

PART VI

Reconciling, Reunions, Research and Writing

Scene 21

Ruth is thirty-six years old.

Ruth: 1965
           'Joe, I'm leavin' with the children.
           You can come or stay, but I'm goin'.'

Image of a low-set, three-bedroom suburban weatherboard home.

           Joe not as keen. Came.
           Died in 1986. Cancer.
           Apologised to the children. To me.
           All individually.
           I told him, too late for that.
           He told me to write it all down. Tell the children.
           Those words. His death – truly set me free.

           My involvement in the community,
           Brisbane Blacks – the Movement, the Cause.
           I saw the move to the city,
           a life that would be filled
           with possibilities for everyone.
           And especially for me and Mother.

           We settled in the northside, close to Mum.
           Ruby Anne always the VIP at every family function.
           Fussed over by everyone there.
           A good grandmother she became.
           The grandchildren loved her,
           called her, Mimi.

Gunggari for 'great grandmother'.
But for Munya and Buthalangi,
the damage was done.
Acquaintances, we'd become.
We never said, 'I love you'.
We never shared a loving embrace.
Our last on that fateful day …
our second separation.

I'm still angry.
I won't except 'The Apology.'
Mother wasn't here to hear it.

*Ruth grabs a piece of cloth, representing the cloth that was ripped
in Scene 3. It has been sewn together – with a machine stitch, a secure
hand stitch and a loose craft stitch (like an X), with a crochet border
around it. We have seen Ruby doing this crocheting earlier in the play.*

Ruth: It doesn't matter how hard you try
           to put somethin' back together,
           once it's broken,
           it's … broke.

She shows the cloth to the audience, emphasizing the stitches.

People try many ways to fix a break.
And the 'trying' is what counts.
The effort to work pass the damage,
to be commended.

Buthalangi and Munya.
Mother and daughter.
Our journey back.
But no matter how hard we try …

Pause.

This piece of cloth will never ever be the same.

Ruth carefully folds the cloth.

And we did, try.

Ruby enters. Ruth hands the cloth to Ruby, their outstretched hands touch, ever so gently.

Ruth: But … I do have a mum.

Ruby: I am your mother.

Image of a Kurrajong tree in bloom fills the back panel that images have previously been projected onto. The shape of a Kurrajong tree canopy emerges. There is a voiceover of Ruby singing in language.

Ruby VO: (Finishing the song sung in language, she chants) 'White man take my baby away … '

'I almost had mine taken away. And that's my daughter today, Ruth Hegarty. She never left me. She never left what she stand for. She's a beautiful woman and dedicated christian.'

Actor 2:   Ruby Anne, as she came to be known,
            she was only to come,
            'For just a little while …'
            'To help her family settle in …'

            Buthalangi died at the ripe old age of ninety-four,
            on the 9th of August 2003.

Scene 22

~ 1996 ~

Ruth, aged sixty-six, back on her chair.

RUTH: Someone arranged a dormitory reunion.
At home, on Cherbourg.
This reunion caused a great deal of excitement.
Us Dormitory Girls maintained that close family link.
I wonder, who would be there from my Dommo
Sisters?
Death had claimed many.

A hundred and twenty of us,
and some of our children.
We reminisced about the old days.
There was little bitterness.
We remember those that had gone.
The day was a great success.

To complete my journey down memory lane …
I begin my walk up to the dormitory,
I remember, it's been nearly thirty years
since I'd last been here.

The building had been unoccupied for a long time.
Renovation being done, to house young singles.
As I approach, it didn't look as … threatening.

I notice:
The paint peelin'.
The once well-groomed garden,

overgrown with weeds.
The six-foot fence gone.
No more barbed wire.
And those thorny roses,
creeping over the ground now,
trying desperately to survive.
There was a touch of sadness about the place,
a stark contrast to its old glory days.

I walk through sawdust strewn over the floors,
which we had once kept so highly polished.
Walking through that maze of rooms,
images flash, rushin' through my mind.
Returning to the scene of my childhood …
tears fill my eyes.

*The distant sound of the nightly prayers. And school lessons. Laughter
and chatter. Crying and fears.*

RUTH: I wandered from room to room,
savouring every moment.
Even entering those once-hallowed places
I once feared as a child.
I had a sneakin' desire to run,
stomp and scream through the hallways.
But I continue, quietly.
With reverence.
I didn't want to desecrate the memories.
To do what I came to do.
One last look.
And I was terrified I might hear,

'Is that you, Ruthie?'

A chuckle to herself. Then, a long beat.

A few months later,
another phone call informed me …
… fire swept through the dormitory.
Burnt it to the ground.

I'm not sure how I feel about that.
They ask –

'When are you gonna to write that book, Ruthie?'

There had to be more information around,
something written down,
some official records of the dormitory.

On advice from one of my daughters.
I went to the Department of Family Services,
Aboriginal and Islander Affairs, George Street.
Hoping to discover some of the Dormitory Girls'
history.

Actor 2 plays a Clerk.

CLERK: 'No.'

RUTH: They said.

CLERK: 'No official history.
           No one expected you Aborigines to survive.
           No one bothered to write a history.
           But … we do have a file on you.'

RUTH: Surprised to say the least.
            'A file? What'd ya mean?'

CLERK: 'Everyone who went through the dormitory system
            has a file. Would you like to see it?'

RUTH: 'Would I like to see it?!'

Clerk hands her the file. Ruth realises what she is holding.

            And as I turn the pages,
            my life, written on official letterhead.

*Projected on the panel are all of the government documents from
Ruth's and Ruby's personal files that appeared throughout the play.*

            Memorandums, letters, copies of travel permits
            and clothing
            dockets.
            Letters I sent to the Department of Native Affairs.
            Wages, stolen. Contributing to the State.
            Letters to me, that I never got.

            Horrified to discover,
            they wrote it all down,
            put in a file, to sit, for fifty years!

            'I don't want my children or anyone seeing this
            (*indicates her file*).
            I want all my files destroyed.'

CLERK: 'They don't belong to you!'

RUTH: 'What do you mean they don't belong to me?
          That's my life's journey written there.'

CLERK: 'They are the property of the Queensland
          Government.'

RUTH: (*Aside*) Oh, here we go again.
          Property of the Queensland Government!
          Still!

CLERK: 'A wavier on your file, well, on some of it, you could
          put.'

RUTH: So, I do!

Memory fades away.

RUTH: Seeing all that information in the file
          made me realise
          how much control they had over our lives.

A little chuckle escapes her.

          How ironic it turned out to be –
          here was material
          I could use to help me write my book.
          But it took the phone call,
          about Dulcie's death.
          Determined Dulcie.
          A paraplegic. Born that way.
          One of us Dommo Girls –
          to get me started.

Ruth sits down in her chair.

I've completed the task I set out to do.

She holds up her published award-winning book, Is That You, Ruthie? *Image of the book cover is also projected – 'Is That You, Ruthie?'– Winner of the David Unaipon Award.'*

Those of us who remain have a livin' history in this book.
It's the truth as we lived it.
It is now complete and comes from my heart.
Whether it is received well or rejected, my hope …

… is that a dormitory girl's story will live on.

Present Day.

ACTOR 2:   Dr Ruth Hegarty, or aunty Ruthie as she is fondly called by the community, has written –
2 autobiographies
1 biography
1 fiction
and seven children's stories.

ACTOR 1:   Her achievements and awards,
just to name a few –
Premier's Award for Queensland Seniors
International Women's Day Award
Local Hero
Centenary of Federation medal
and honoured with a Doctorate in Letters.

ACTOR 2:   For a little Dormitory Girl,
           Ruth defied all the odds,
           and lives her long life with grace and determination.

ACTOR 1:   With over 150 descendants.

ACTOR 2:   She fulfilled her promise to her Dormitory Sisters,
           as well as seeking constantly to expose
           the wrongs imposed on her and her people.

Projected on the panel is a series of photos of Aunty Ruth Hegarty: one speaking, in her Doctorate robe and hat, a beautiful portrait of her younger self.

ACTOR 1:   She's an Elder.

ACTOR 2:   An Activist.

ACTOR 1:   An Author.

BOTH: And a Queensland Great.

Image – a portrait of a beautiful smiling Ruth.

Acknowledgements

Is That You, Ruthie? The Play was first produced by Queensland Performing Arts Centre (QPAC) in association with Oombarra Productions at Cremorne Theatre on 2 December 2023, with the following cast:

Actor 1: Ruth (Munya)	*Melodie Reynolds-Diarra*
Actor 2: Ruby (Buthalangi)	*Chenoa Deemal*
Writer & Director	*Leah Purcell*
Movement/Choreographer	*Jeanette Fabila*
Set & Costume Design	*Chloe Greaves*
Lighting Designer	*Ben Hughes*
Composer & Sound Designer	*Will Hughes*
Video Designer	*Justin Harrison*
Design Associate	*Ben Mills*
Design Coordinator	*Wendy Rix*
Dramaturg	*Alexander Bayliss*
Stage Manager	*Pip Loth*
Production Manager	*Kylie Mitchell*
Executive Producers	*BainStewart*
	Oombarra Productions &
	Jono Perry, QPAC

A heartfelt thank you:

To my ancestors who give guidance and walk with me every day.

To my family – Bain, Manda, Raf and Lysander, and Odi the dog – for your love, and for the freedom and support you give me to pursue my dreams.

To Aunty Ruthie, the Duncan and Hegarty families; a special mention to Moira and Becky Bligh.

To the original creative family (cast and crew) who helped to bring this production to fruition – always grateful and appreciation to you all.

To the QPAC team, including John Kotzas AM, Jono Perry, Kate Driscoll-Wilson and Bradley Chatfield.

To Kathy Frankland – Community and Personal Histories/ Culture and Economic Participation at the Department of Treaty, Aboriginal and Torres Strait Islander Partnerships, Communities and the Arts (DTATSIPCA).

To Desmond Crump – Language Consultant and Translation, Dhinawun Consultancy.

To University of Queensland Press for supporting the publication of this play, and the creative input and insight into bringing it to fruition.

To my team at Creative Representation, thank you for your belief and support. A special mention to Wendy Howell, my literary and directing agent.

And a big thank you and big love to my partner in movement, my sista Aunty Jeanette Fabila. Sis, your calming presence, spiritual nurturing, good yarns, contagious laughter and skill are so appreciated.